FUN·TO·LEARN

MY

BODY

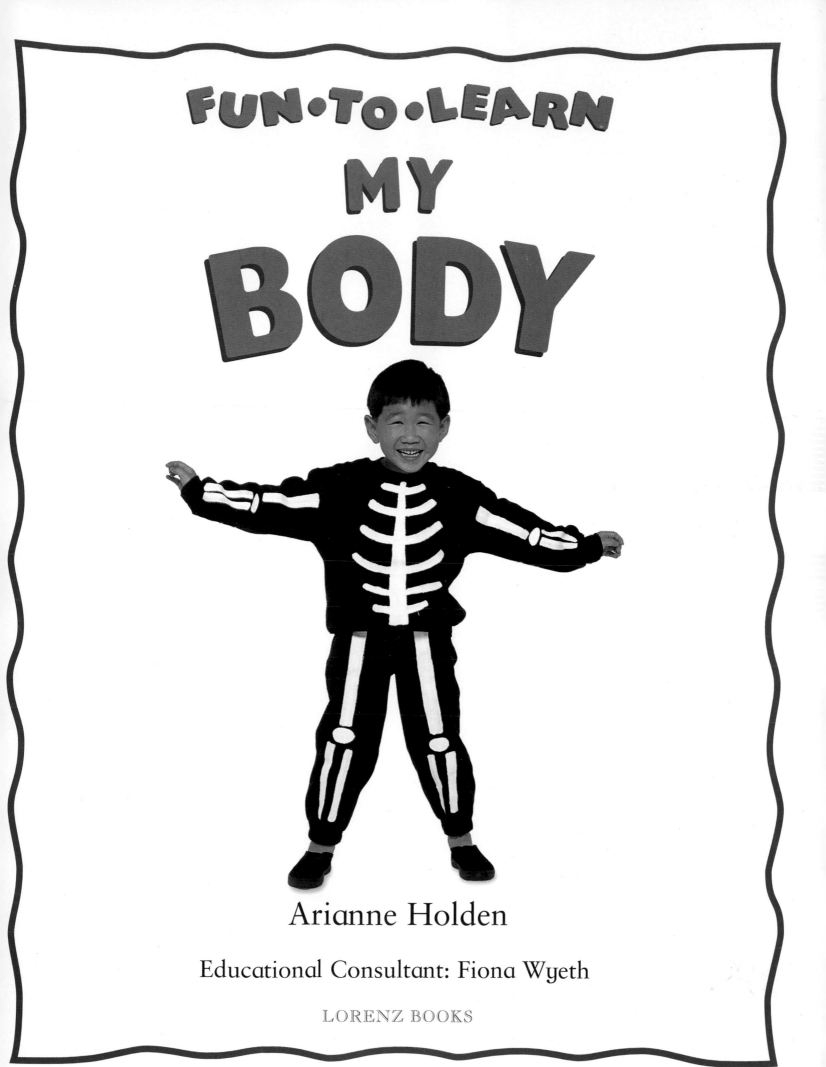

Arianne Holden

Educational Consultant: Fiona Wyeth

LORENZ BOOKS

NOTES

Fun to Learn About My Body helps children to understand their body and the way it works. Informative text, lively photographs and plenty of fun activities and experiments ensure that children learn in the best way of all—by doing.

Reading together

Children benefit from adult help when reading a book. Do not expect your child to grasp all the information at once! Focus on one concept at a time, and allow a few days for the information to be absorbed before moving on to a new topic.

Talking it through

Talk about the things you have found out together. Make everyday activities an adventure in learning. Meal times provide a perfect opportunity to talk about teeth, taste, tongues and healthy food, while an outdoor play session is a stimulus for discussion about what the body can do.

Answering questions

Ask your child questions and encourage him or her to answer. Do not worry if the answers are wrong—making mistakes is part of the learning process. The most important thing is that your child has the confidence to answer.

Checking your child's understanding

You can check your child's understanding of how the body works by asking questions like, "Why do we get tired? Why do we exercise?"

Learning by doing

Encourage your child to try the activities in this book. They have been specially devised to be easy and fun to do. They will also help your child understand that it really is fun-to-learn!

CONTENTS

Look in a mirror. Do you look like any of these children?

Your body

Everyone is different. You are the only person who looks exactly like you.

head

This is the front of my body ...

... and this is the back.

shoulder

arm

hand

neck

Your body has lots of different parts. All the parts have special names.

waist

hip

thigh

knee

leg

foot

4

two long,
strong arms

five toes

five toenails

a round bottom

Point to Anna's eyes, nose, mouth and cheeks.

five fingernails

one thumb

four fingers

ankle

wrist

heel

5

Bones

Inside your body are your bones. Without them, you would be like a wiggly jellyfish.

That is what I look like inside.

There are lots of small bones in your hands.

Bones fit together to make your skeleton.

When you cross your legs ...

When you lie down ...

... your bones look like this.

... your bones look like this.

You can feel hard bones in your ...

... skull

... knees

... and elbow

6

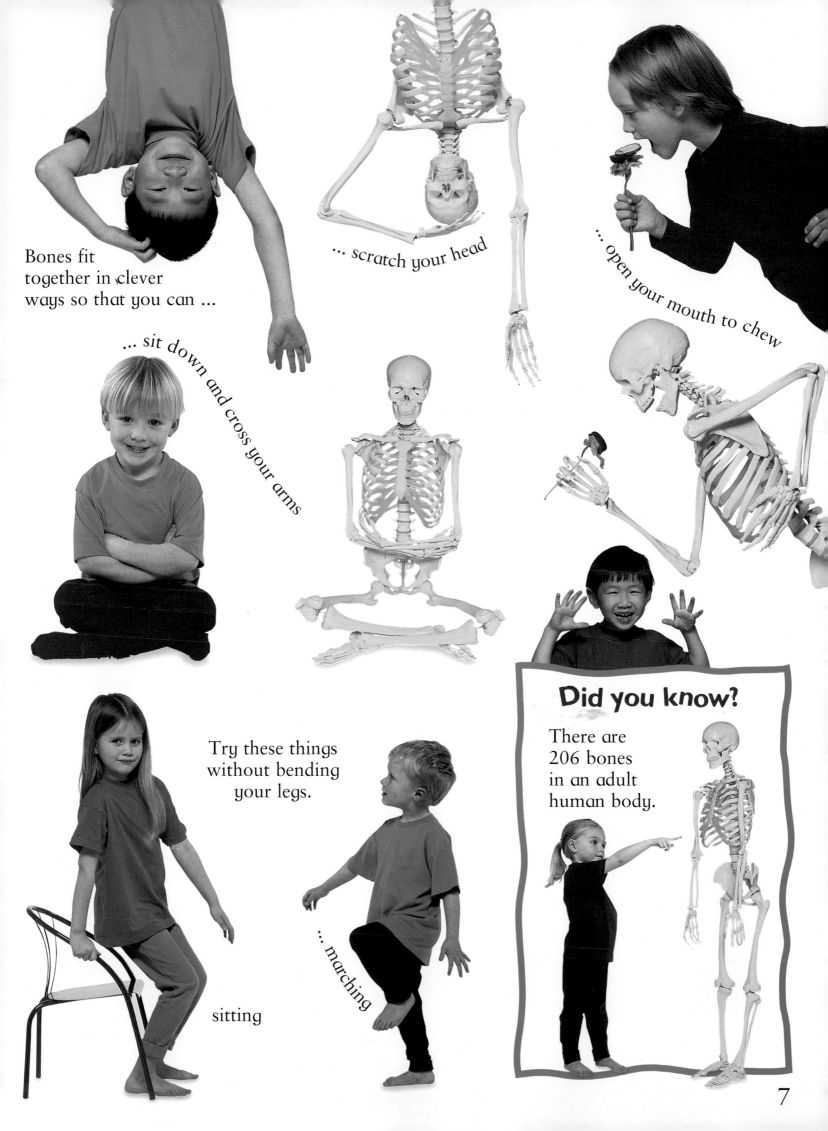

Bones fit together in clever ways so that you can ...

... scratch your head

... open your mouth to chew

... sit down and cross your arms

Try these things without bending your legs.

sitting

... marching

Did you know?

There are 206 bones in an adult human body.

7

Muscles

Your body uses strong muscles to help you do amazing things. Your muscles are under your skin.

Strong muscles help you lift things.

hula hoop spinning

Flexible muscles let you move around.

gymnastics

leaping

jogging

You use the muscles in your face to make a ...

... funny face

... balloon face

... fish face

... monster face

Lungs

When you breathe, air goes into your lungs. You need air to live.

This is what your lungs look like.

Feel yourself breathing.

Your lungs...

... stretch like this bag when you breathe in and ...

... shrink when you breathe out.

Heart

Your heart is a muscle. It pumps blood around your body.

This is what your heart looks like.

Try this!

See your breath

Stand close to a mirror and breathe on it. Your warm breath will mist the mirror.

Have you ever ...

...cut yourself ...

You can listen to a heart beating.

thump ... thump

You can feel blood moving through your wrist.

...or had a nose bleed?

9

Skin

Your skin protects your body and keeps your insides inside!

Do you get goosebumps when you are cold?

When you get hot you sweat to cool down.

Your skin is waterproof.

You should protect your skin from the sun.

Try this!

Fingerprinting

1. Color a fingertip with a magic marker.

2. Press it onto a piece of paper.

3. Look closely to see the wiggly lines.

Your skin is soft and flexible.

Your skin is covered with tiny hairs. The hairs help you stay warm.

Growing

You are growing all the time.
You even grow when
you are asleep!

Babies grow into ... young children ... older children ... and then into adults.

Try this!

Make a height chart

Stand in front of a piece of paper
taped to a wall. Ask a
friend to mark your height.
Wait a month before your height
is marked again. Have you grown?

fingernails

Fingernails
and toenails
grow all
the time.

My hair grows longer every day ...

... but I like mine short!

toenails

Eat up!

Your body needs healthy food and drink to keep it working.

I eat lots of healthy food!

Your body needs lots of fruit and vegetables.

Potatoes ... bread ... pasta ... rice ... ... will give your body energy.

Did you know?

You need 7 cups of water every day. Some of this water comes from the food you eat.

fish

nuts

cheese

Your body needs these foods to make it strong.

eggs and milk

beans

seafood

These foods are yummy, but don't eat too many of them.

Teeth

You have hard teeth inside your mouth.
They chew food so that it can be swallowed.

Front teeth cut and slice.

Back teeth squash and grind your food.

Babies have just a few teeth so ...

... they can only eat mushy food.

You can eat all sorts of food.

Brush your teeth to keep them clean and shining.

Try this!
Toothy impressions

1. Ask a grown-up to cut a slice of cheese or apple.

2. Take a big bite out of the cheese or apple.

3. Look closely and you will see how your teeth have cut through the food.

Taste and tongues

Your tongue is a muscle that helps you to taste your food. Taste is one of your five senses.

There are tiny bumps on your tongue ...

... called taste buds.

Can you feel your taste buds?

I love strawberry pudding ...

... but I don't!

Your taste buds tell you if food tastes good or bad.

Everybody likes different tastes. Do you like to eat...

... hot dogs?

... cake?

... juicy grapes?

Would you like to eat these foods?

purple pasta

blue carrots

red bread

blue mashed potato

green fish sticks

blue french fries

silver peas

Try this!

Taste and tell game

1. Put some of these foods on a plate. Your friend must not see the food.

salty cracker

sweet, juicy apple

crisp lettuce

tasty cheese

spicy sausage

creamy yogurt

2. Blindfold your friend. Feed them each different food.

3. Can they name each food?

Can you do these things with your tongue ...

... roll it?

... touch your nose?

... lick your chin?

Smell and noses

Your nose tells you what something smells like. Smell is one of your five senses.

Have you ever smelled a flower?

Tiny hairs in your nose help you to smell things.

Do these things smell good or bad?

talcum powder

sweaty shoes

lunch box leftovers

...yesterdays socks

rotten egg

hot chocolate

Try this!

Taste test

1. Half-fill four cups with water.

2. Add fruit juice to one, lemon juice to another, and a little salt to the third. Leave the fourth cup as is.

3. Blindfold a friend and get them to pinch their nose closed. Ask them to taste and name each drink.

They won't be able to name the drinks because they can't smell them.

These things can make you sneeze.

dust

dogs

cats

hay

rabbits

guinea pigs

pollen from flowers

feathers

When you have a cold, your nose is stuffed ...

... and you can't taste anything.

Does anything make you sneeze?

Ahh choo!

17

Touch

Your skin helps you to feel the things around you. Touch is one of your five senses.

A rabbit's fur feels soft and smooth.

What do you think these things feel like?

cloth

bear

balloons

pudding

pineapple

lizard

Oh no!

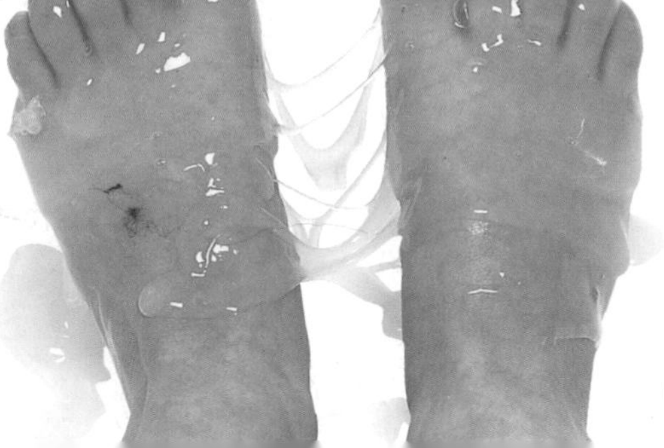

slime

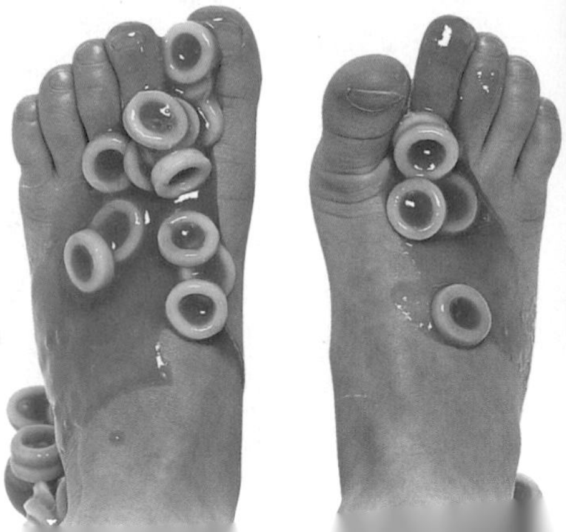

noodles

1. Find 7 things that feel very different. Put them in a bag.

bark

feather

lollipop

bath sponge

cookie

metal dish

stuffed animal

Try this!

Touchy feely game

2. Ask a friend to feel what is inside the bag. Can they name the things without peeking?

Some parts of our bodies tickle when they are touched.

Where are you ticklish?

Can you tell what someone looks like by feeling their face?

You can feel if something is warm or cold with your ...

... hands

... lips and tongue

... or feet.

Take care! Never touch very hot things—they may burn you.

Hearing and ears

Your ears help you to hear all the sounds around you. Hearing is one of your five senses.

What can Ben hear?

two friends telling funny stories

a noisy airplane zooming across the sky

his blue clock going tick-tock-tick-tock

a fast car ... vrooom!

a hungry kitten meowing

his favorite music

Sound can travel along a string.

You can make sounds **louder** with a megaphone.

Can you he*ar* me now?

What sounds do you make when you ...

... smack your lips? ... blow a raspberry?

Have you heard these musical instruments?

trumpet

recorder

saxophone

maracas

tambourine

drum

Some children wear hearing aids ...

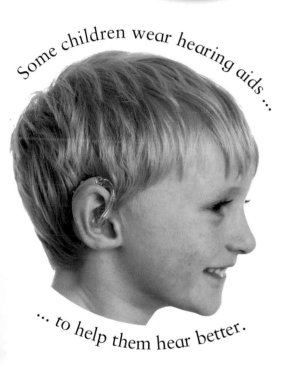

... to help them hear better.

Try this!
Crazy orchestra

Make funny sounds by blowing bubbles in a glass of water, banging bowls and waving a big sheet of cardboard.

Make some annoying noises.

pop bubble wrap

pop
pop
pop

grind your teeth

grind
grind

eat noisily

crunch
crunch
crunch

21

Sight and eyes

Your eyes help you to see everything around you. Sight is one of your five senses.

Look in a mirror. What color are your eyes?

blue

a pair of beautiful green eyes

blue-gray

gray

brown?

Try doing these things with your eyes closed.

painting

Did you know?

Blind children read books by feeling little bumps on the page. Their alphabet is called Braille.

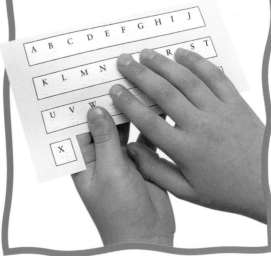

eating

putting on gloves

Glasses help you see better.

A magnifying glass makes things look bigger.

Swimming goggles will protect your eyes.

Can you find the ten differences between these two pictures?

Your eyes can show how you are feeling.

Try this!

Put the tail on the puppy

1. Paint a puppy and a tail on cardboard or paper. Cut out the tail.

2. Put an inside-out loop of tape on the back of the tail. Tape the puppy to a wall.

3. Blindfold a friend. Spin them around three times. Ask them to put the tail on the puppy.

grumpy

silly

sad

Keeping healthy

You need to take care of your body to keep it working well.

You can keep your body fit and healthy by ...

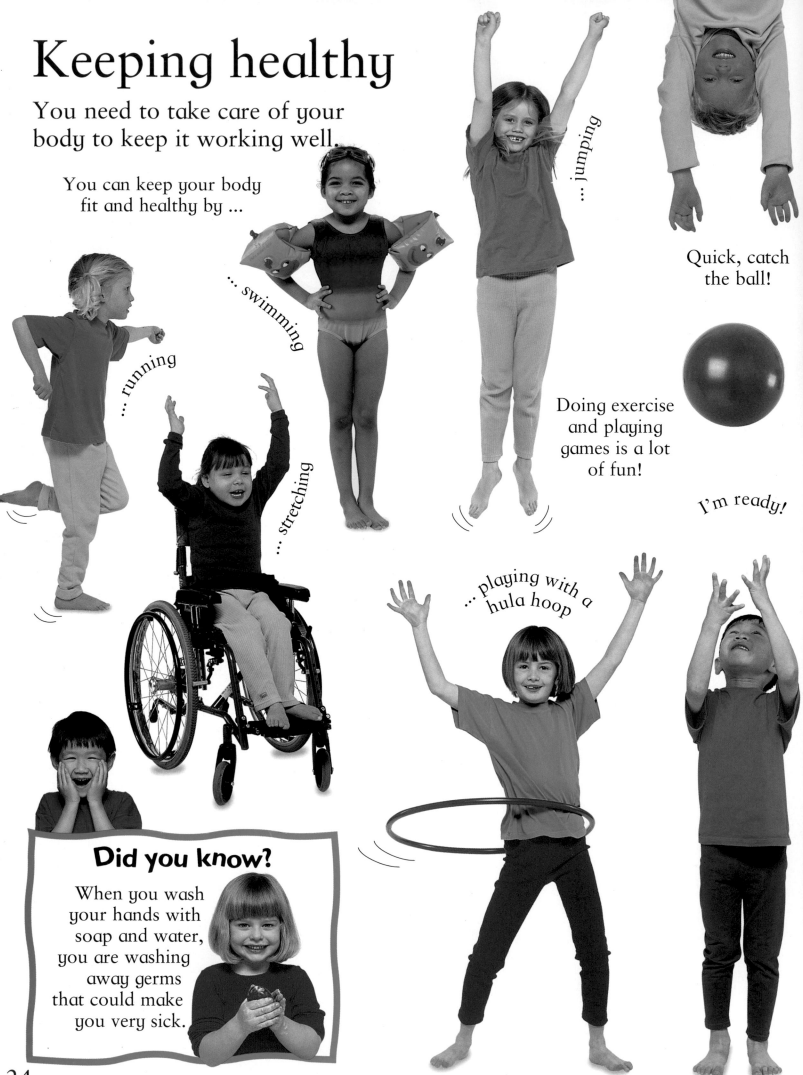

... running

... swimming

... jumping

... stretching

... playing with a hula hoop

Quick, catch the ball!

Doing exercise and playing games is a lot of fun!

I'm ready!

Did you know?

When you wash your hands with soap and water, you are washing away germs that could make you very sick.

24

A bad cough can be caused by germs.

Sue has a cough and now all her friends have coughs.

A handkerchief can help stop germs from spreading.

flying germs

cough!

cough!

cough!

To be healthy you have to ...

... get plenty of sleep

... and eat healthy food.

If you are sick and have to stay in bed, a grown-up or a doctor may ...

... give you medicine

... take your temperature

... ask you to drink water.

Let's talk

To let others know how we feel
or what we need, we talk.

mmm

ssss

Can you
make these
sounds?

th, th, th

ahhh

oooo

Place a hand on your throat
to feel sounds being made.

Sing "ooo" and change the shape of your mouth.
What happens to the sound?

hello
hello
hello

ooo

eeeee

Sounds can be soft or loud.

quiet whispering

Cover your ears to make loud sounds quiet.

loud shouting

Try this!

Talking with your fingers

Use your fingers to spell out the word "talk" instead of saying it. This is called sign language. It is used by some children who are deaf or who are unable to talk with their voices.

t   a   l   k

We can talk by making signs with our body.

Do you know what these children are saying?

Brain power

Your brain is in control of everything that your body does. Your brain is working even when you are asleep.

Your brain is inside your head, but you cannot see it.

Your brain is good at thinking. It helps you to...

... build models

... do jigsaws

... read

Here are tricks you can play on your brain. Move your nose towards the two fish.

What happens to the little fish?

Hold a finger in front of your nose and close one eye. Place another finger in line behind it.

Open your eye. Are both fingers in line?

28

Try this!

A memory game

1. Place ten things from around your home on a plate.

2. Ask a friend to look at them for one minute. Cover the plate.

3. How many things can your friend remember?

You even need your brain to do simple things.

laughing

eating

While asleep you sometimes dream wonderful stories. Have you ever had a dream about ...

... being a famous dancer?

... being a superhero?

... being chased by a dinosaur?

Copy cat game

Roll a dice and move markers to see which actions you have to copy. You can play this game by yourself or with friends.

START

Are you ready to move into action?

markers or buttons

dice

1

2

3

Bend down and touch your knees five times.

4

5

6

7

Time to get marching.

16

Jump as high as you can.

15

14

13

12

10

8

9

11

Do five jumping jacks.

17

18

19

20

21

22

23

24

25

26

27

28

29

30

31

32

33

34

Throw and catch a ball five times.

Jog once around the room.

Close your eyes and balance on one leg.

Spin a hula hoop or wiggle your hips like a hula dancer.

Well done! Time for a healthy drink.

FINISH

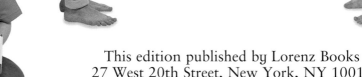

This edition published by Lorenz Books
27 West 20th Street, New York, NY 10011

LORENZ BOOKS are available for bulk purchase for
sales promotion and for premium use.
For details, write or call the sales director, Lorenz Books,
27 West 20th Street, New York,
NY 10011; (800)354-9657.

Lorenz Books is an imprint of Anness Publishing Inc.

ISBN 1 85967 833 5

Publisher: Joanna Lorenz
Managing Editor, Children's Books: Sue Grabham
Project Manager: Lyn Coutts
Educational Consultant: Fiona Wyeth MA, BEd
Design: Mike Leaman Design Partners
Photography: John Freeman
Head Stylist: Melanie Williams
Stylist: Ken Campbell

The Publishers would like to thank the following children for modeling in this book:
Irene Agu, Rosie Anness, Kari-Ann Barbe-Parker, Harriet Bartholomew, Jonathan
Bartholomew, Daisy Bartlett, Kitty Bartlett, Ambika Berczuk, Chilli Bernstein, Andrew
Brown, April Cain, Milo Clare, Callum Collins, Matthew Ferguson, Rubin Fox,
Luke Fry, Safari George, Saffron George, Zaafir Ghany, Lana Green, Billy Haggans,
Miriam Nadia Halgane, Madison Harrington, Faye Harrison, Lily Haycraft Mee,
Charlotte Holden, Eve Howard, Daniel Jackson, Alice Jenkins, Kadeem Johnson,
Zamour Johnson, Daniel Kelleher, James Kelleher, Sumaya Khassal, Cleo Kinder,
Otis Lindblom Smith, Holly Matthews, Jack Matthews, Rebekah Murrell, Philip
Quach, Tom Rawlings, Ashley Read, Olivia Risveglia, Eloise Shepherd,
Giuseppe Sipiano and Kayla Valcin.
Note - an adult skeleton was used on pages 6-7.

Printed and bound in Singapore
© Anness Publishing 1998
Updated © 1999
1 3 5 7 9 10 8 6 4 2